STOCK MARKET INVESTING

INVESTING

By Dexter Jones Jr.

Table of Contents

CHAPTER I:
Introduction

Many people get confused between a Stock
market and Financial Market and think that
they are the same, but they are not the same.
In simple terminology a Stock Market is a
place where stocks are traded. Very simple
definition isn't it? It is a place where a seller
sells a stock to a buyer via the platform
provided by stock exchange through

computers. The transaction or trade is done during specific hours on business days which are normally from Monday to Friday. Though it may look simple from outside, the answer to this simple question is more complicated than one might think. Some traders trading for several years still would not be able to give you a proper definition or exact nature of transactions that happen in a stock exchange. Through this book, we are going to clear the ambiguity, and give our readers a direct and succinct explanation to what happens in a stock exchange and how you can gain by investing in it.

CHAPTER 2: How Do Stock Markets Function

A stock market is not very much confusing as it is normally made out to be. There are investors like small time businessmen, housewives, Walmart store-boys who have invested in stock exchange and made profits. Stock market is a place where investors can buy or sell shares of a particular company. The primary objective of all the investors is to get the maximum return on their investment.

This sounds very logical. To do this, a stock

or share has to be purchased when the price is

low and sold when the price goes up. The

margin or the difference between what you

paid to get the share and the money you made

by selling the share is your profit. So,

obviously you can increase your margin by

increasing the number of shares you buy and

sell. You might think that this sounds like a

walk in the park, but it is not because

investors who are confused by stock markets

lose their money than making profit. So, it is

not only better to understand but also, beneficial to understand what a stock exchange is and how it works.

From the perspective of a nation, a stock market plays a vital role in helping large companies raise capital for their operations and gain access to an alternative stream of capital apart from loans and company revenue. Stock markets are platforms that provide the opportunity to traders to make profits by speculating on the price of shares. Clever traders can predict the stock market behavior and anticipate stock price trends across particular companies or even industry sectors. Remember, that stock market allows the free-flow of trade in shares without the need for physical presence or negotiation of contract terms. This is the very essence of a stock market.

Shares are instruments just like your Dollar bill which enable the free transaction from one trader to another without the need for registration of the sale deed. In simple terms, you are making a sale without the need to register the transaction which would have made the whole thing time consuming. Such trades or transactions are the lifeblood of several growing public companies. Above all, a sign of a growing economy is a strong stock exchange. So, on the whole, a stock market operates by creating a platform for buyers and sellers of shares to meet and exchange their shares. Stock markets trade in real-time throughout the business day with the help of a broker, who executes the trades automatically on demand. The trader engages in active speculation throughout the trading period. Normally, a broker will buy a share for the trader which is expected to perform well in the future. The term speculation means that a thing may happen or not happen. So, the factor of risk is always present along with huge returns. The sale of the share is made when the trader feels that it will not perform anymore and that its price has peaked and would not go any further. At this point he will instruct the broker to act on his behalf and sell the shares. A stock broker, as in the case of a real estate broker, acts on behalf of the trading party. A trader or an individual cannot enter a stock exchange to perform the trade but has to do it via a registered broker. In this sense, these stock

markets provide an ideal opportunity for

determined individuals and trading

organizations to invest and reap profits.

CHAPTER 3: Why You Should Invest In Stocks

Ever wondered why Bill Gates still makes it to

the top of the Forbes richest every year? Well,

rich people have built a system that will

generate money for them even while they are

sleeping. Their portfolio of investment, in

other words, the collection of places where

they have invested is done in such a way that they will generate money consistently over a period of time. What can we learn from people who have made money and fortunes that are enormous by any standards?

Income earned from monthly salary is essential to most of the people to sustain their livelihood in the society. We invest so much of our time and energy when we are young to acquire professional skills in order to use them to earn a healthy income. This means our professional knowledge is our main asset that we possess when we join the work force.

However, this professional skill is not just our best weapon in the professional world but also that of others; meaning several others who studied along with us or worked with us do own these skills just like us. And this dents our bargaining power in the industry. So, our professional skill is not a mantra that can take us to the paths of riches. Every year thousands of fresh graduates come out of colleges and universities. So, what should you do to stay ahead?

Earning money from paycheck or salary is not a proven way to become rich because it depends on what job you are doing and where you are working. Not everyone is a CEO of a top level company. For those who work as a clerk or technician without any extra perk, it is very difficult to become rich. So, the only way to become rich is by investing money in stocks or shares of companies that are performing well. If you are saving money out of your salary and keeping the money in a savings account, you are not going to get much of an interest on that savings to leap-frog your financial status. But if you have a good savings you can buy shares of companies in a prudent manner and hold on to it till the price rises to a point where you will feel comfortable to sell it off for a good profit. You can even use these shares to get dividends on a long run. In that case, you can earn dividend and then sell the shares in future for a good price. Many people have used this method to pay the college fees of their children or to pay the down payment of their new apartment. The money will always be put to good use if you have a plan in your mind. It will not go waste.

Many people join sales teams and commission agencies to increase their income. Sales agencies work like pyramidal hierarchy system. Once you reach the top of the pyramid hierarchy, you will receive a part of your down level sales commission. This can increase your income but tell me how many people living near your home have made money by ranking high in the pyramidal hierarchy system. Very few and the best examples are fast dwindling. Besides, deviating your focus from your sole income stream and investing your time on sales will lead to losing your job. Many people have fallen victim to this. They did this mistake of investing plenty of time to climb up the pyramidal hierarchy system to earn money at the cost of their day job. Remember what I wrote earlier about rich people; they need not be physically present or even be awake to earn their money. Sales commission cannot be earned without your presence to negotiate with a prospective client and following up with them. Your presence and skills will be tested while negotiating on the price and terms of the deal. On the whole, you are the one who can make the deal happen and "You" need to be physically and mentally present to do sales. None of this is needed to earn money from a stock exchange. You are sitting in front of your desktop or laptop using your own intuition and knowledge to pick up company shares which you deem fit. You may be watching CNN Money or reading the Financial Times while investing in stock exchange. The leisure is all for you to experience.

Now, let us go back a step and see how you should invest money. This is very crucial because if you keep doing what you are doing

and still not lose money that is a safer bet than

investing it in stocks and losing money. So, let

us learn the basics of how to invest and not

lose money. Ready for the Gyan?

CHAPTER 4: How Should You Invest In Stocks

This chapter is going to be a little lengthy but

I will make it an easy read for you. This

chapter contains the key mantras to investing

in stock exchange and I am giving special

focus on where to invest depending on your investment goal.

First, you have to decide the purpose of your investment. Are you looking at returns from investment on a yearly basis or post retirement returns or need a corpus just before retirement. Plan it before you take the next step. Once you have taken the decision on the purpose of your investment, you will have avoided the first mistake that most people make while investing in stock market.

Now let us take each scenario into consideration. Let us assume that you want to

use the stock investment to generate income.
The income that is generated from stocks is in
the form of dividends. Let us learn more
about it.

Income from Dividends

Dividends are payments that companies pay
out to their stockholder. This depends on the
performance of the company on a year to year
basis and each year, the rate of dividend will
change. By holding a stock or share, you
become an owner of the company. So, the
company that is operating with your money
will have to pay you a fee for using your

money for its operations. This fee is called dividend. That is the technical part.

For each share you own in a company, the company will pay you an amount which is normally less than a Dollar for each share. So, the more share you own, the more your dividends.

Let me help you with an example. Let's assume that you own shares in a company that are valued at $20 each. You invested $1,000 in total. This means you own 50 shares of that company. The company decides to pay a dividend of $0.20 each quarter (three months). This means the company will pay you $0.20 per share times 50 shares. You will get $10 each quarter from the company. The more share you own, the more dividend you will get. Remember that a company is not obliged to pay dividend and they are not a guarantee, but it is a nice perk with a company that has a long history of maintaining and raising dividends. These are also called Blue Chip stocks.

Normally, the money that's paid as dividends is deposited in your account with your stockbroker. However, you can instruct the stockbroker to deposit that money to your bank account. Remember that the dividend money that you receive each year or quarter is in addition to the normal value of the share. Quite obviously, companies that pay their shareholders a healthy dividend will have more valuable stock than companies that don't ever pay a dividend. So, whenever you sell the shares of a company that pays dividend, you will get a better profit than from those companies that don't pay dividends. Many large investors live life of riches by receiving money from dividends.

They would own a huge number of shares of a company and the return that they get will naturally be very high. Well, we haven't reached that stage yet but we have taken our baby steps in that direction. What we are doing here is to slowly build up on your day job income to a point where your day job income can be completely set aside for savings or other investment.

Investing for Retirement

Investing in stocks for retirement is a very good way to make use of your today's income. Many people look at stock markets as a way to make investments that will give them a nice retirement. If that's your goal, you should consider using a 401(k) plan at work in conjunction with a Roth IRA. Your savings account is not going to give you much returns that will help you live a lifestyle of today in future after retirement. This is one main reason why many Americans have taken the stock investment route via 401(k) plan. Like I wrote earlier, income from day job is not sufficient to take you to the next level of financial status. That can happen only if you invest in instruments like stocks or bonds or try investing in real estate.

Employers nowadays offer a 401(k) plan that allows employees to invest their pre-tax income into a special brokerage account. In this account, you'll have investment options suited for the size of investment you are planning to make. In future, when you have retired, you can take money out of your 401(k) whenever you wish. When you pull out your investment, you can pay a tax and withdraw all your money. Unlike a 401(k) plan a Roth IRA is a retirement option that doesn't require a plan from your employer. The employers do not have to match your contribution to this plan. You can open an account with any investment firm. The only difference is that unlike a 401(k) plan where you do not have to pay taxes initially, in a Roth IRA, you will have to pay taxes initially. However, at the time of withdrawing money from a Roth IRA at the time of retirement, you do not have to pay any taxes.

Investing for Speculative Trade

I am not a big fan of speculative trade but there are many people who have made money by just predicting the manner in which the stock market would react. Let us assume that you have $10000. You believe that a company Trans International Inc. that is valued at $60 per share will see its share price go up in the next week. You buy 100 shares of this company for $6000. The next week, just as you predicted, the share price goes up to $63. This means your total stock value is $6300 instead of $6000. You have made a profit of $300 in a few days. The more stock you have the more profit you make.

Speculative trade has many flipsides as well. Just like many people have made money in the short run, many have lost money due to their lack of spreading the risk factor. Spreading the risk factor means one should not put all your eggs in one basket. If you predict that a company share will perform well and put all your money in that stock, that is a great risk. What if the company shares do not increase or worst if it goes down? So, you should spread your money across various kinds of companies. Shares of companies that are technology startups will fluctuate too much. This can go up or down by a substantial margin. Let us say, if LinkedIn, which is a public company is having a negotiation with a company like Microsoft for acquisition, then naturally, the share price of LinkedIn will go up. However, the price of its share will go down the moment the deal goes down the drain. So, speculation with technology startups are risky but if you play your cards smart, you can make money too.

Stocks like Apple Inc. or Microsoft, GE or Oracle etc. will not go up all of a sudden. They are strong companies with super strong fundamentals. Their stock will appreciate only by a small margin over a period of time. If you are buying shares of such companies, it is better to hold it for 10 or 20 years before selling it for a fortune.

How your money will shape up in future will depend on your decision. The purpose of investment will help you take a decision on where to invest. Your decision on where to invest and what stocks to buy will in turn make or break your fortune. A person who invests in stock market just because his office peers are investing or his boss has invested in stocks will not have a clear purpose for investment. Such people tend to lose money and become living examples of those who have burned their money in stock markets.

Remember, while you are planning for an investment, you are stretching your mind and working out the possible scenarios that you will face in future. You will be planning things like when to marry, how many kids you should be having, where you are going to buy your new house and things like how much to save for retirement etc. Stretching your brain over these crucial things will itself have a positive effect in your life. So, when you are taking a decision on what should be the purpose of investment, you would have already decided on how you want to live 20-30 years from now. This is why I suggest that you take time to decide on the purpose of your investment in stock market.

CHAPTER 5: Stock Market Investment Procedure

Now that you have decided to invest a small sum of money into stock market, let us see how much of a small amount is a small amount to invest. Brokerage firms, just like any other financial firms will have a minimum investment requirement. So, if you are planning to invest with $250 or $300, chances are that you might be asked to increase your investment fund. You would have noticed the usage of share and stock in this book. Most companies will not allow one or two shares to be purchased. They will ask you to purchase a lot of 10 or 20 or even 100 shares. A bunch of shares is called a stock. When you approach a stock brokerage firm, they will obviously ask you for a minimum investment as well as ask you to buy a certain number of shares of a company. So, in most likelihood, one cannot go for investment in stocks with small amount of money.

Stock brokerage firms are of two types: full-service and discount. A full-service brokerage firm provides a gamut of service to its customers like providing advice on where to invest, mapping the share price trend etc., but unfortunately, such service is reserved only for high net worth clients who can invest anything above $100,000. It is very common to see minimum account sizes of $50,000 or up at full-service brokerage firms. Don't be disheartened because there are discount brokerage firms that do not need a hug investment from you. Discount brokerage firms have lower fees, but they will not advice you on where to invest and when to sell or buy. They will most likely not pick up your call if you call them with stock market queries. Their fees are very low because you are in charge of your investment decisions.

With a small investment, you can however purchase shares directly from a company via their direct stock purchase plans (DSPPs). Though every company has a minimum purchase requirement, you can still buy shares for a sum of $500 or $1000.

Fees and minimum purchase requirements are kept by brokerage firms and companies because they have administrative costs which can be recouped only if the purchaser of

shares makes a prescribed minimum

investment. This is the same scenario as in

banks where you have your savings account.

So, don't think that such restrictions are only

in brokerage firms.

If you are finding it hard to take a decision on

which company to invest, you can purchase a

Mutual Fund plan from a brokerage firm.

These mutual fund plans are also sold via

banks. Mutual funds, like the name suggests,

are investment vehicles which are managed

by a team of fund managers who invest on a

portfolio of shares. There is a fees associated with mutual fund investment and due to this reason, there is a minimum lock-in period for your investment. This means if you have purchased a mutual fund, you have to continue investment till a specific period of time until you are eligible to withdraw your money. This is due to the administrative costs associated with managing the mutual fund. The fund managers of mutual funds have to be paid a salary to keep them working so the fees associated with a mutual fund is normally high. However, there is a specific minimum guaranteed return from a mutual fund plan. So, you won't end up making a fortune but your investment will give you more returns than your bank savings scheme. Many people prefer mutual funds due to its risk free nature.

Brokerage Commissions and Fees

Just like mutual fund fees, a brokerage also charges commission or fees for using their services. Remember, investing in stocks can be very costly if you trade frequently since for each trade you have to pay a brokerage fees. So, if you have a very small investment amount, you may find it difficult to buy shares. Every time you trade, you will incur a trading fee. This is a fee that you have to pay your brokerage firm for providing you the services or platform for trading. Imagine you buying a website domain name from a domain registrar like GoDaddy. You own the website but every month or year you will have to pay a fee for the domain registrar for providing you with the services. Trading fees or brokerage commission typically range from the $10 per trade, but sometimes can be as high as $30 for some discount brokerage firms. A trade is an order from your end to purchase shares in one company. This order is made to the brokerage firm. So, naturally, if you want to purchase many stocks at the same time, they will all be seen as separate trades and you will be charged a commission for each one of the orders or purchases.

Let me give you an example. Let us assume that you decide to buy stocks of five companies with a sum of $1,000. To do this you will incur $50 in trading costs. So, if you invest the $1,000 completely, your account would be reduced to $950 after reducing the trading commission. This represents a 5% loss even before you have earned any return on your investment. So, don't trade often because you will incur commission costs each time you trade. Remember that, if you were to sell these stocks, you will once again incur trading costs, which would be another $50. So, you have already lost $100 for just buying and selling the stocks. Just by buying and selling the shares you have incurred a cost of $100. If you do not sell for a very good price then your cost of $100 will not be recovered and you will end up losing money.

Opening An Account With a Brokerage Firm

A brokerage firm has access to the stock exchange. For this they would be registered with a stock exchange and would have fulfilled the criteria specified to become a registered stock broker. They will take your instructions and go to the stock exchange and buy or sell stocks according to the instructions you gave. You are actually paying a fees to them for doing your orders. When you open an account with a brokerage, you will be asked to deposit a sum of money with them by transferring it from your savings account.

Once the money's there, you can ask them to buy a certain number of stock you want. Let me give an example; let us say, you want to buy $100 worth of Microsoft stock. You can directly give this order which is a very simple order. You can also give more complex instructions, for instance, you can give a standing instruction to buy 50 shares of Microsoft when it goes below $40 per share. The brokerage firm will exactly do this and charge a fee for following your order. The same way, you can also give a standing instruction to sell stock when its value goes down a specified level. You can consider the brokerage firm as your partner in a stock market who does exactly what you instruct it to do for the consideration of a fee.

Brokerage firms will also have expert advisors who have plenty of experience in dealing with stocks. Their advice may sometimes be available to only investors who spend a big sum of money but nevertheless you can try to seek their advice if that is available small investors. The fee that a brokerage charges for each trade is their revenue. That is how they make money.

Sometimes you would have a query on which brokerage firm to choose. There is no good and bad brokerage firms. You can speak to the public relations officer of brokerage firms to know exactly what they can offer you. This way you can select the brokerage firm that will serve your interest better. Remember, don't pretend in front of the brokerage firm like you are going to invest big money if your initial investment will get you good return. They are brokerage firms and would have seen rich losing money and the poor making it to riches.

CHAPTER 6: Diversification To Cut Losses

As you take your baby steps towards investing in stock market, you will hear many terms that are new to you. One that is notable would be "Diversify" or "Diversification". This in simple terms means that you must diversify your investment and spread your risks. Let us go dep into what it means and how it is done.

Let us assume that you have invested only in the shares of airline companies. Suddenly, the airline pilots publicly announce that they are going on an indefinite strike that would lead to all the flights getting canceled. The share prices of airline companies will go down and you will lose money. However, if you had invested part of your investment in technology companies or renewable energy companies, you would not face this scenario of massive loss. Only part of your portfolio would be affected and chances are that your loss on the airline stocks will be compensated by a rise in the price of shares of companies in renewable energy sector. This is the benefit of diversification. To know how to balance your portfolio, you must keep yourself aware of the latest developments in the technology and corporate world. If a top executive of a company resigns suddenly, the share price of that company will come down momentarily. If the trend follows, the downfall in share price will be a trend in itself. So, be aware of the happenings in the business world.

Similarly, due to global warming and climate change, many countries are promoting green technology. This means if you invest in shares of green technology companies, your prospects of making a profit is higher. But don't invest all your money in green technology companies since if the research that these companies are doing fails to pay off, then the company will go down and its share price will nose-dive.

A balanced portfolio also means that you will have to invest a good amount of money. Without investing a decent sum of money, you will not be able to buy stock of companies in various sectors. It is also important that you spread your risk among different kinds of assets. By different assets I am referring to shares, bonds etc. Bonds don't react the same way as a share. A Bond is more or less an instrument that says that the company owes you a sum of money upon the maturity of the bond. A bond is also traded and its fluctuations are much less compared to that of a share. So, apart from spreading your investment in shares, you can also spread your investment in asset classes. A combination of assets will reduce your risks from market swings.

A question that many people have asked me is how many stocks they should hold across various industry sectors. There is no ideal number of stocks that you should hold across industry sectors. A set of 10 stocks across various industries is better than 5 and a set of 100 is better than 10. The more diverse your portfolio, the better you can absorb the shock from a downfall in stock prices. Remember that there is no guarantee that you will make profit if you have a diverse portfolio. The best that a diverse portfolio offers is a cushion from the shock of falling share price. You can research a company in detail, such its promotors, their background in business world, what all business they have done in the past etc. All these information will help you pick up the stock of a good company. But this doesn't mean that the stock of that company will go up just after you purchased it. However, if a company has good fundamentals and cash reserves like Apple Inc., Microsoft or GE, then they will not go down like house of cards. You will eventually see an appreciation in their share price over a period of time.

CHAPTER 7: Mastering Your Investments

This chapter is going to be a little technical but

I promise to explain the investment strategies

to you in a very easy. In this chapter, I will elaborate on the first step towards investment, which is choosing the stock of a company. The fundamental question is which company's share should be chosen over others. Are there any particular foolproof strategy to choose a company? How many shares should be purchased and many other similar question. Let us take them one at a time.

To invest in stock market, you will have to first choose which company's stocks has to be purchased. There are hundreds of thousands of companies that are listed in stock markets.

You can trade shares of companies that are listed in stock exchange. You cannot trade in shares of companies that are not listed in a stock exchange. For instance, Dell is a famous maker of personal computers and Michael Dell is a household name in the world whose story is as inspiring as that of Bill Gates and Steve Jobs. However, if you want to trade the shares of Dell, you cannot, since it is not a publicly traded company. It was once publicly traded but as of 2013, it is a private company and its shares are not available for the public for trade and speculation. So, you might wonder how a big and strong company like Dell could be a private company. But that is a fact. Facebook is a popular name in the social media space but it became a public company only a few years ago. So, while picking the stock of a company you have to keep in mind a lot of factors; the first one being if that company is public or private. As the name suggests, you can buy and sell shares of public companies and cannot trade in the shares of private companies.

The next important aspect to study is the strength of a company in terms of its valuation and price of share. Before I go ahead, let me remind you that if you are looking at speculative trade and want to make money in the short run, this valuation of share and all things as such might sound fluff. You will say, "Hell, why should I care what the real share value is? All I am concerned is how much I can sell if for."

So, my advice to you is if you are looking at long term profit, then you might consider looking at the intrinsic value of a share. A company is valuable its owners or promotors can take out money left after operational costs, this in other words called profit. So, if the company has future profits, then its intrinsic value is high. That is why companies like GE has high intrinsic value since they have won contracts for the next 4-5 years and this will give them immense profits. However, companies in the oil refining sector will see its stocks going down when the price of oil is down globally. To be a smart investor you have to factor lot of things like these. You will also have to look at the growth rate of the company for the last 3-5 years and the projected growth rate for the next 3-5 years, how the media has covered this company in recent times, any class action lawsuit against the company, any litigation against the company by its competitors claiming infringement of copyright and theft of proprietary software. All the above can affect the image and reputation of a company and reflect the same on stock price. An old saying goes that if a promotor sneezes, his company's stock price will be affected.

Check Out For Qualitative and Quantitative Factors

Before I go deep into this, I want to warn you that data is easy to fetch but what data points are relevant is very difficult to predict. There is no thumb rule on what data will help you and what will not, but if you go over all the probable aspects, your chance of making a mistake will be reduced. That is a guarantee from me.

Qualitative aspects are those that are not measured in numbers such as goodwill of company, educational qualification of management team, efforts to make inroads into new markets, behavior of the management team in public are all factors that can affect the share price though they cannot be measured in numbers. You will have to consider these factors very closely. Remember the former CEO of Enron using the "F" word on a conference call with fund managers when asked why his company cannot come up with a Balance Sheet after earnings? Well, these are not signs of good management and obviously the company is history and doesn't exist anymore. These are qualitative factors that you must consider before picking stocks in a company.

The quantitative factors are many and you don't have to be an expert in management to learn it. Quantitative factors include growth rate for the next 5 years, the dividends declared for the last 2 years, EBIDTA, profit margin for the last 2 years etc. are quantitative factors. These are mentioned in the company's annual report and you can access it via the website of that company. A company also has to file a copy with the SEC, so the same can also be found in the website of SEC. There are also websites that does a quantitative analysis of company performance and puts all those figures in their websites. These websites mostly help investors in stock picking and you will find them helpful in arriving at stocks that meets your expectations. A strong company with sound fundamentals will have their management team behaving in a prudent manner both in and off public. They will not comment out of the way on issues that are political or religious. A sign of good company is a stable management team. The GE Chairman and CEO has been serving his company for around 20 years and his predecessor Jack Welch served the company for 20 years. These are signs that the company is in good hands. If you find that a company is doing management reshuffle often, it is best to avoid purchasing their stock. Likewise, if a top executive who has left the company files a case against the company then wait for some time for things to cool down before planning to purchase their shares.

On the quantitative aspect, there are a few things to consider apart from the numbers. If a company's profit percentage is consistently falling quarter to quarter, please do check the numbers for other companies in the same industry. If you find the same trend, then the fall in profit is normal. For instance, oil industry will have a fall in their profit when oil prices are down. This is a global phenomenon and almost all the oil companies in the world will see a reduced profit during this period.

In today's world, technology companies appear and vanish every quarter. They also bring about technology disruption that can sometimes break the rhythm of an existing industry. For instance, if you have invested in a company that offers taxi service, you will find the company's business going down after the entry of Uber in the market. This is not because the taxi service provided is not doing business properly, but because the parameters and yardstick which existed before Uber came into the business has changed ever since Uber's entry into the market. This is called disruptive technology. Many taxi service providers have lost business since Uber made an entry into their market.

New product releases can also increase the share price of a company. For instance, when Apple Inc. releases new versions of iPhones, the share price goes up because of investor confidence going up due to the product becoming a hit. You would have seen media news channels showing the long queues in front of stores waiting to grab the new product. All these factors increases the share price of Apple Inc.

Investing When The Economy is Down

If you are stepping out of your comfort zone to invest in stock markets at a time of economic downfall, you are not doing a mistake. Many people think that it is good to trade only when the economic activity is good and when the US is doing well in all aspects like employment and GDP. This is not true.

Many people make a fortune by buying shares when the economy is down and hold on to it till the prices go up. They sell the stocks when the prices are high. Imagine buying stocks during the recession of 2008. You could have purchased more shares during recession than during economic upswing. So, eventually when the economy shows signs of recovery you can wait for a chance to sell. When the prices have increased and stabilized, you can sell them for a huge profit. This is very much similar to real estate investment where people with money will go on a buying spree when real estate prices are very low. They will buy

assets everywhere and spread their risks.

When the markets recover, they will reap

profit by selling them. So, economic downturn

is an opportunity that can be utilized well if

you act wisely.

CHAPTER 8: Conclusion and A New Beginning

Words in this book will not help everyone to become rich but it surely will help you get the confidence to take your first step towards an investment which is proven to make people rich. If you have decided to try the stock market, then take home a few advice. Before you invest, make sure that you have a good backing because your investment will not reap benefits in a month or two. Ideally, if you and your spouse are working, then it will be good if you both have earmarked an amount that you plan to invest in stocks. If you both have taken that decision, then setting aside $10000 or $ 20000 won't be difficult. This much of money is a healthy sum to upstart your investment. Also, if there is a chance that you will have to depend on your family's income till the returns start arriving, then keep everyone in the family informed that you are going to invest in stocks and that it normally takes some time to get back the investment and make profit. This way, no one is going to come asking you every now and then that how much more it is going to take before you start making money. However, if you don't have anyone to answer to, make sure you have a self-discipline that will help you. Try not to do what the crowd is doing. Somedays you will have an office colleague asking you why you missed investing in a particular company. Such incidents are bound to come up. But be disciplined enough to have faith in your ability to pick a stock. You have made a decision to pick a stock based on your qualitative and quantitative analysis. You have checked media reports about the company and also did a study of the industry the company is operating in. If you have picked out a company's stock to invest after factoring all these parameters, then you have made the right decision.

Remember that you started off by taking a decision. You started off by taking a decision on why you want to invest in stocks. Taking decisions is very crucial. Whether you are in your 60s, 50s or 30s, taking a decision on what you want to be and how you want your money to be used will make or break you. All the celebrity businessmen, film stars and sportsmen that you can name made it this far

because of that one thing called "Decision".

So, decide today that you want to be better

financially in the next 5 years, decide that you

want to invest your savings in such and such

companies, decide that you will use the profit

for a purpose that you had predetermined.

You have made it even before you started !!